Hopping Online

by Refried Bean

Hopping Online

by Refried Bean

Introduction

Hi, my name is Refried Bean. I write stories and poems and publish a lot of books for young people. This is a collection of designs using images from a computer program called Canva. Most of the creatures were designed by other artists, and I used the graphic design software to create scenes and images for a picture book that I thought children might like.

Many of my books are for any ages, but I think this one is for very young children who also might like to have the stories in the back of the book read to them. I guess that is different than normal picture books, but it helped me use the space in the book without running out of memory on my computer.

Thanks for reading this book. I hope this work does not get wasted, and even though it is a team effort using new art technology, it is some of the most fun I have had creating books.

God helped me with my life, and I hope he helps you too, whoever you are, whichever friend accepted this gift from me.

Acknowledgements

Thank you Howards World, Dolly Parton,

Precious Longdoggie and sister Angel Pippy,

Thank you Nadia from Amazon,

Thanks, Venmo, Paypal, and Citibank.

This book is dedicated to Beth and Wendy.

5

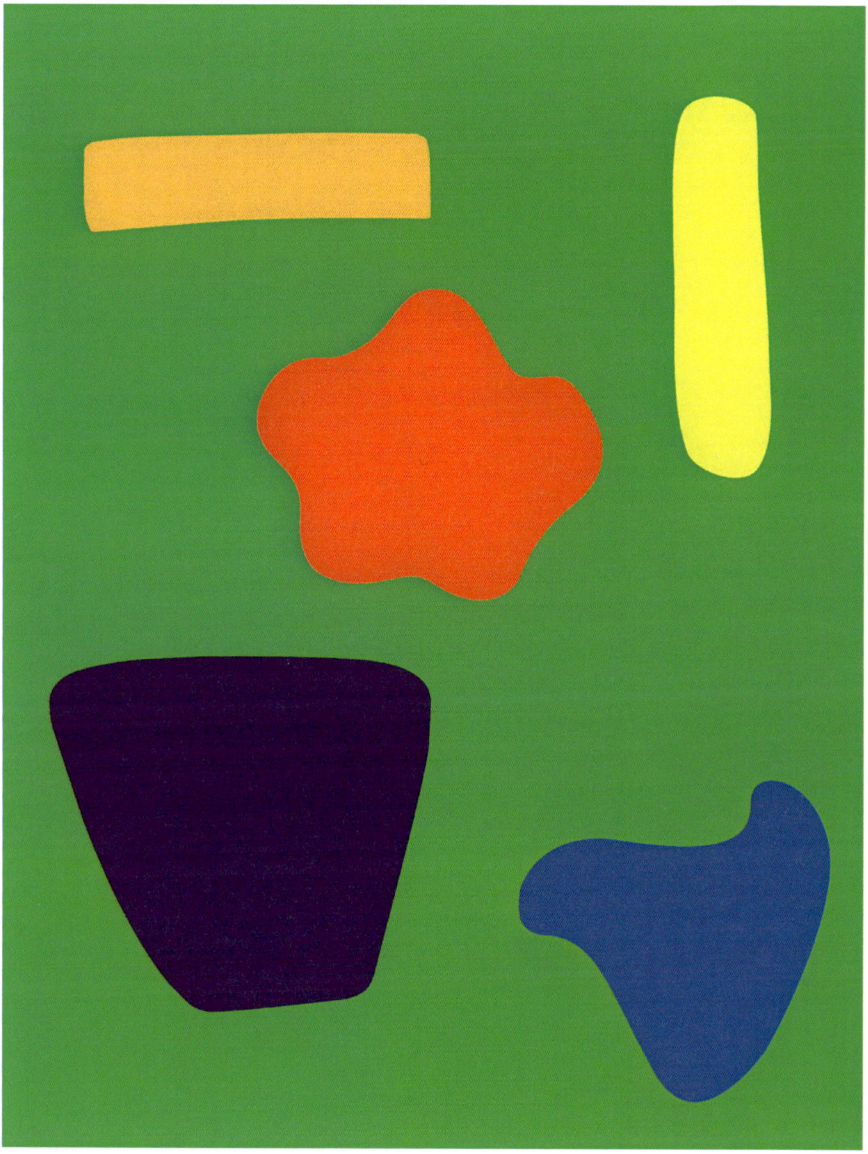

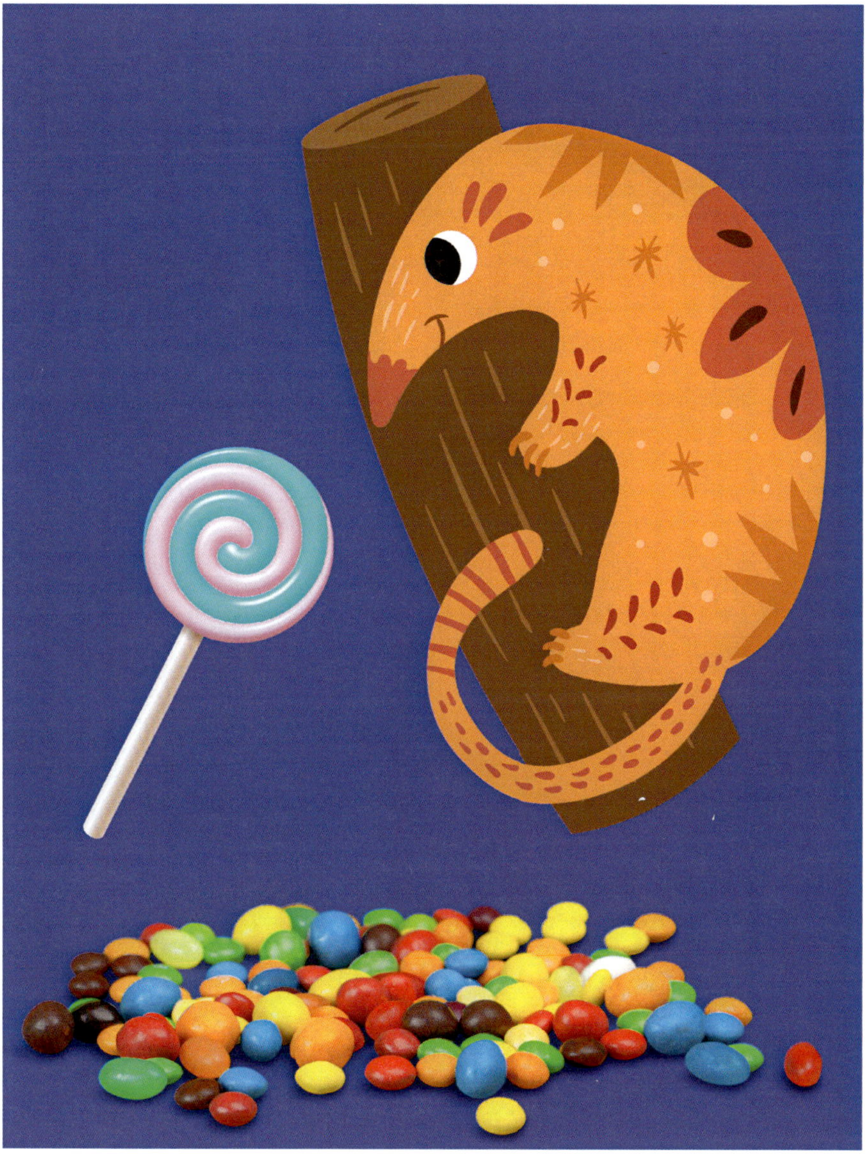

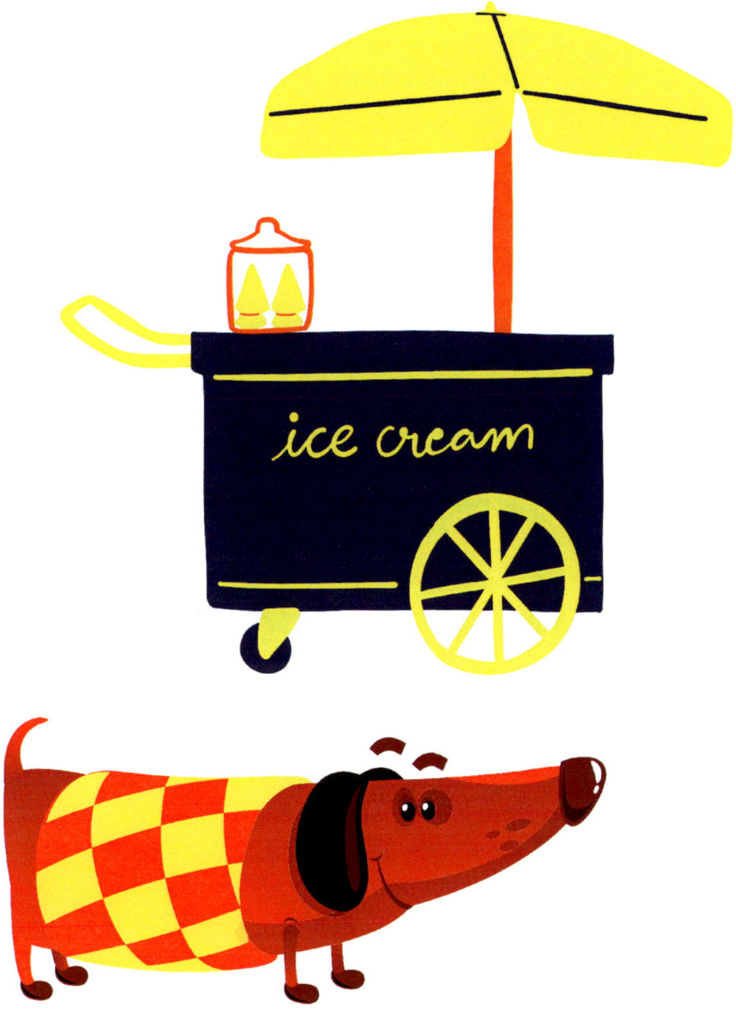
ice cream

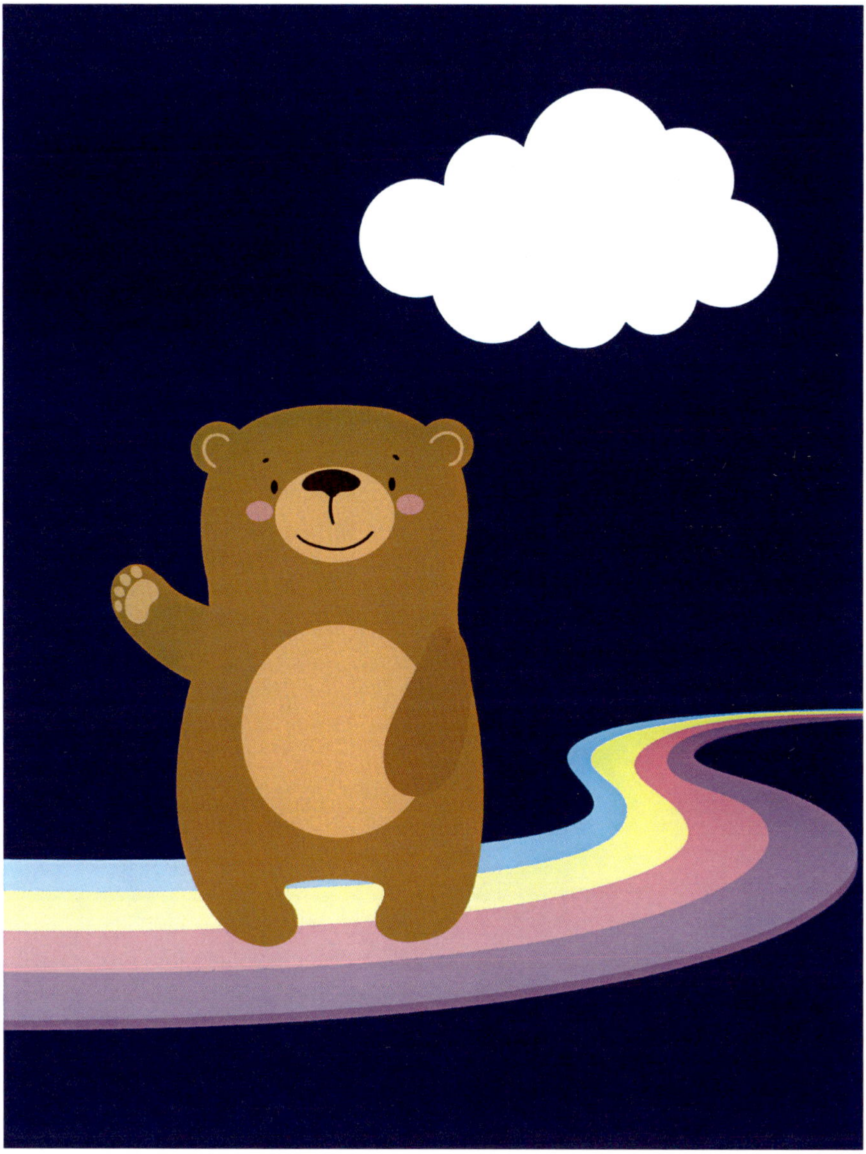

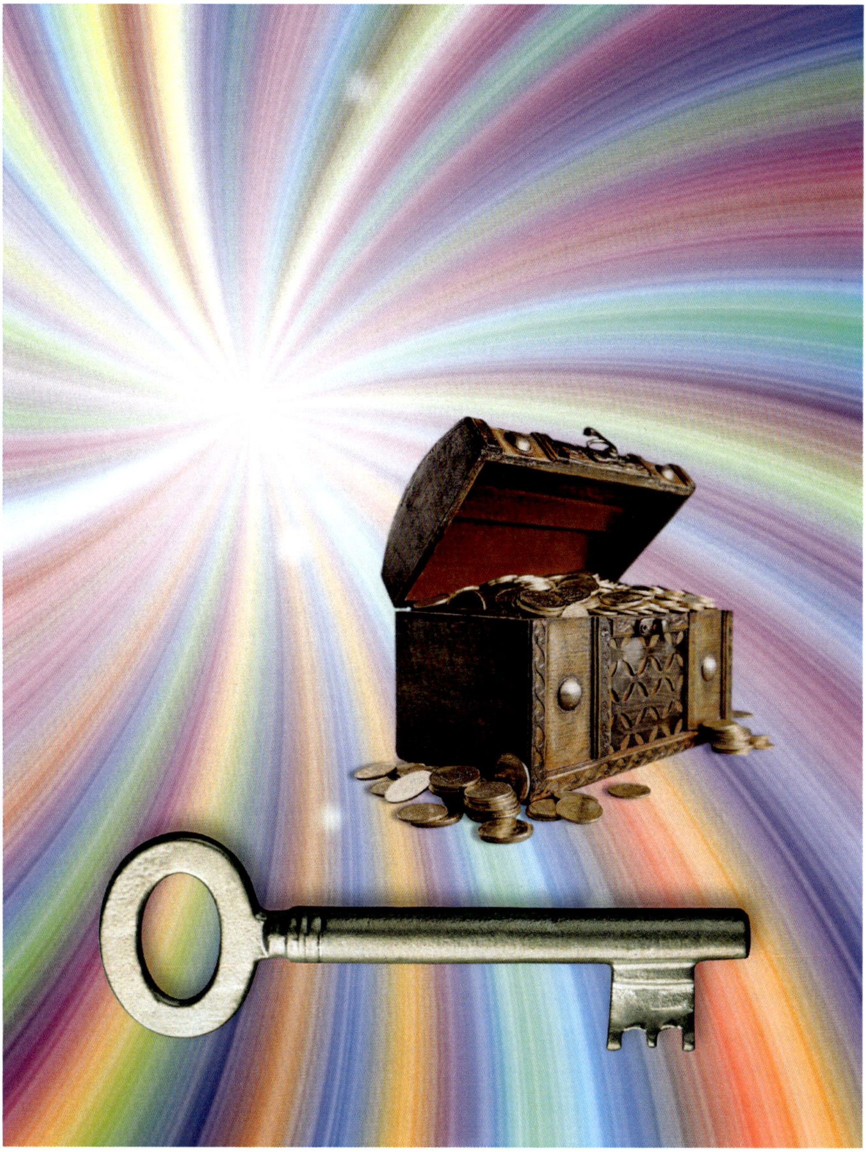

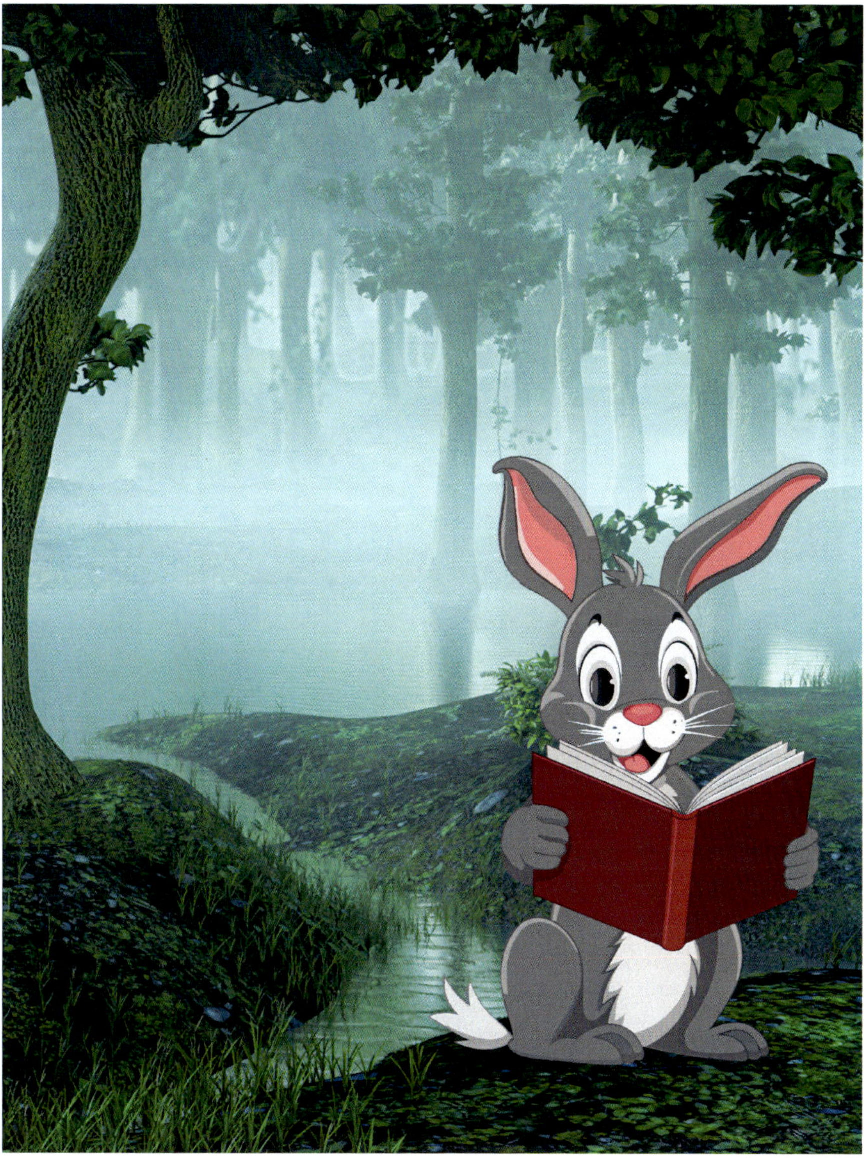

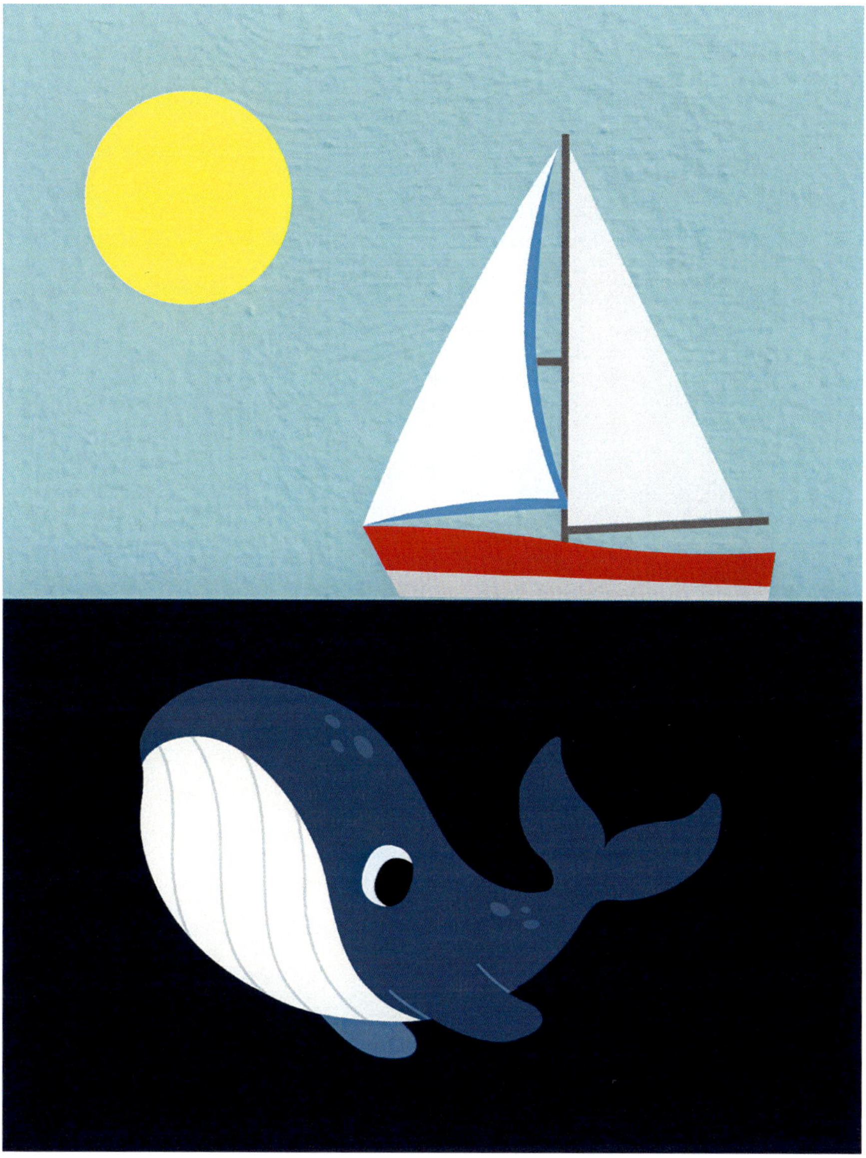

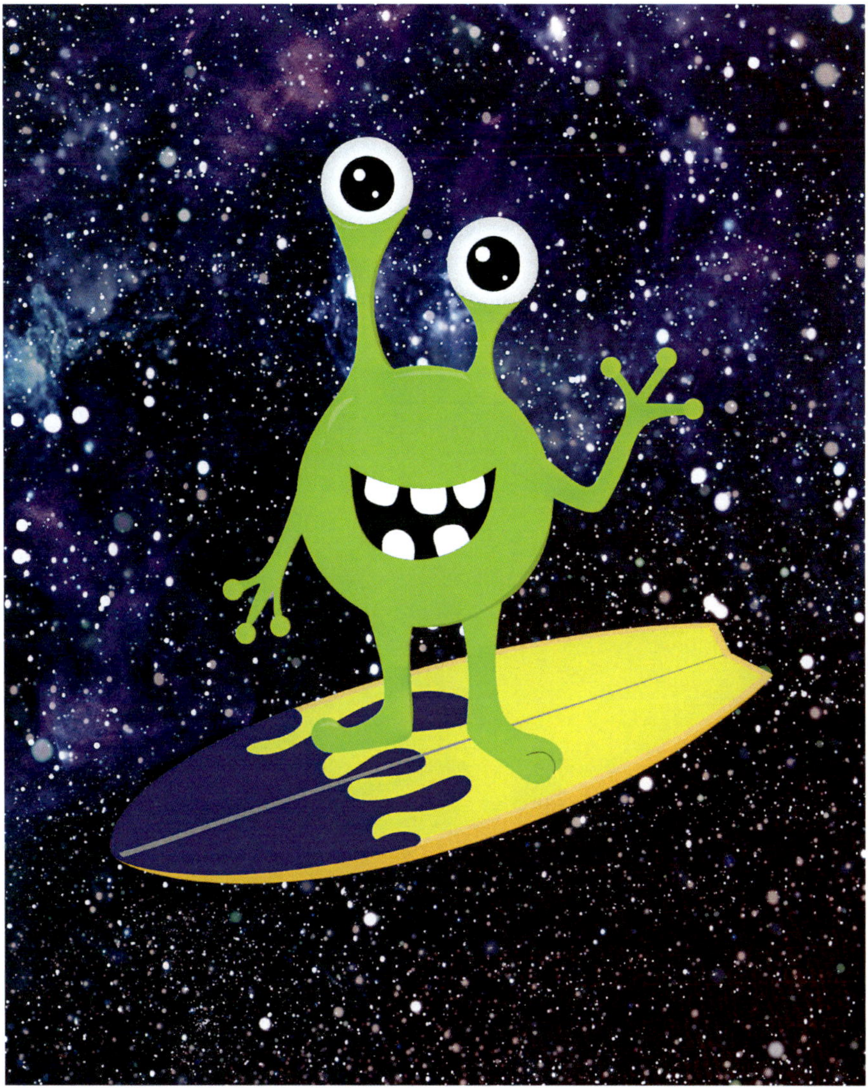

23

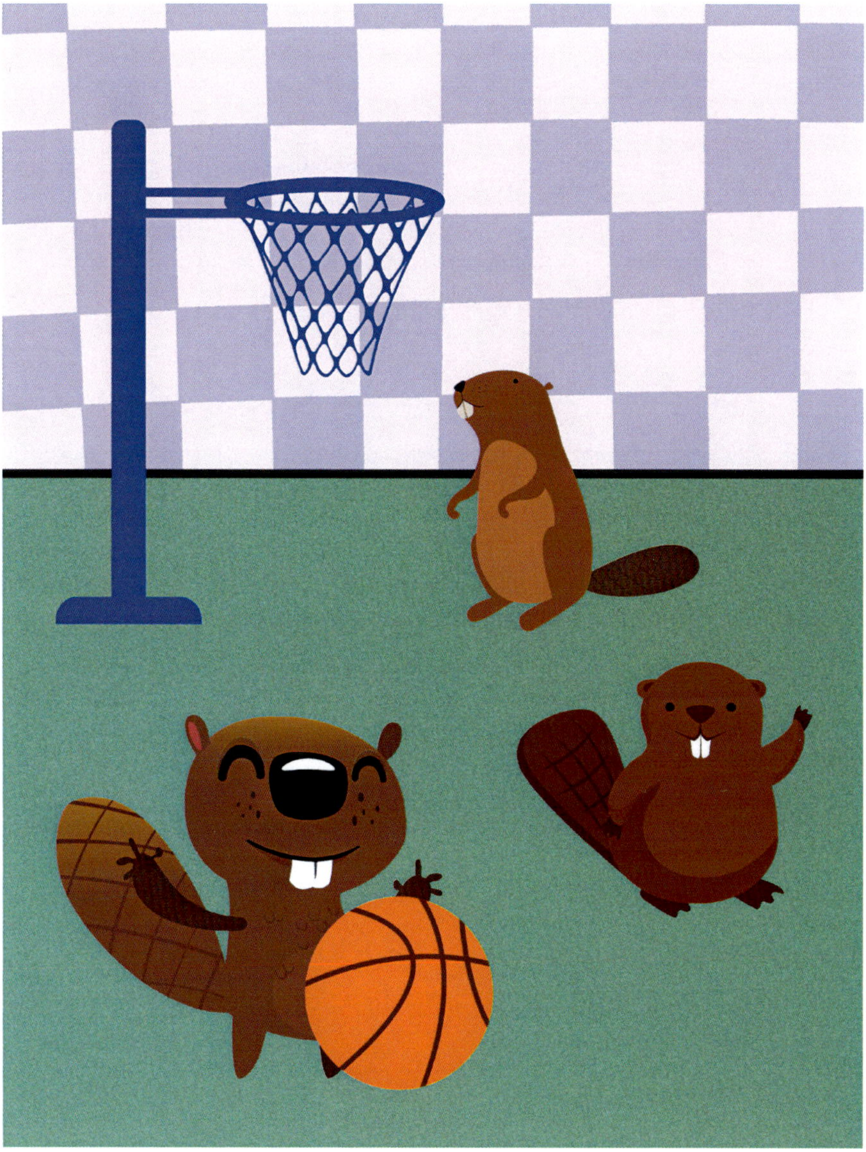

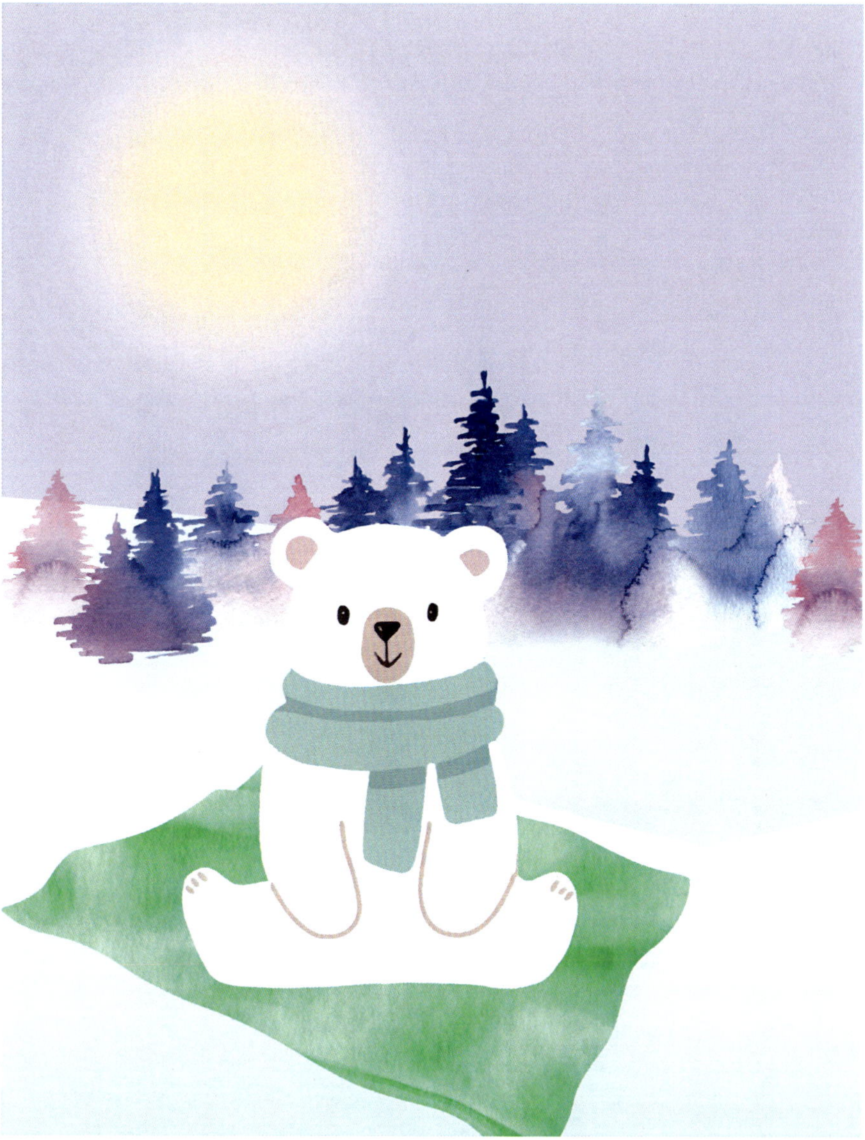

ICE CREAM

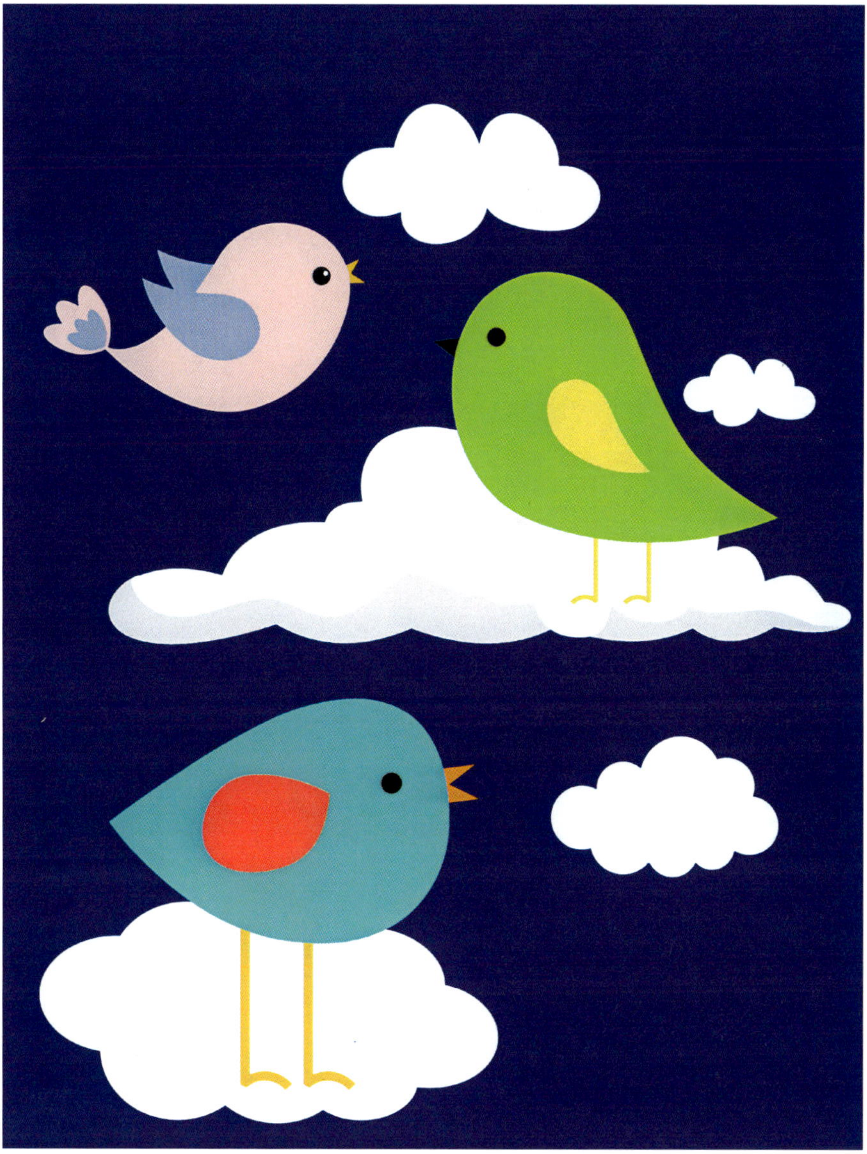

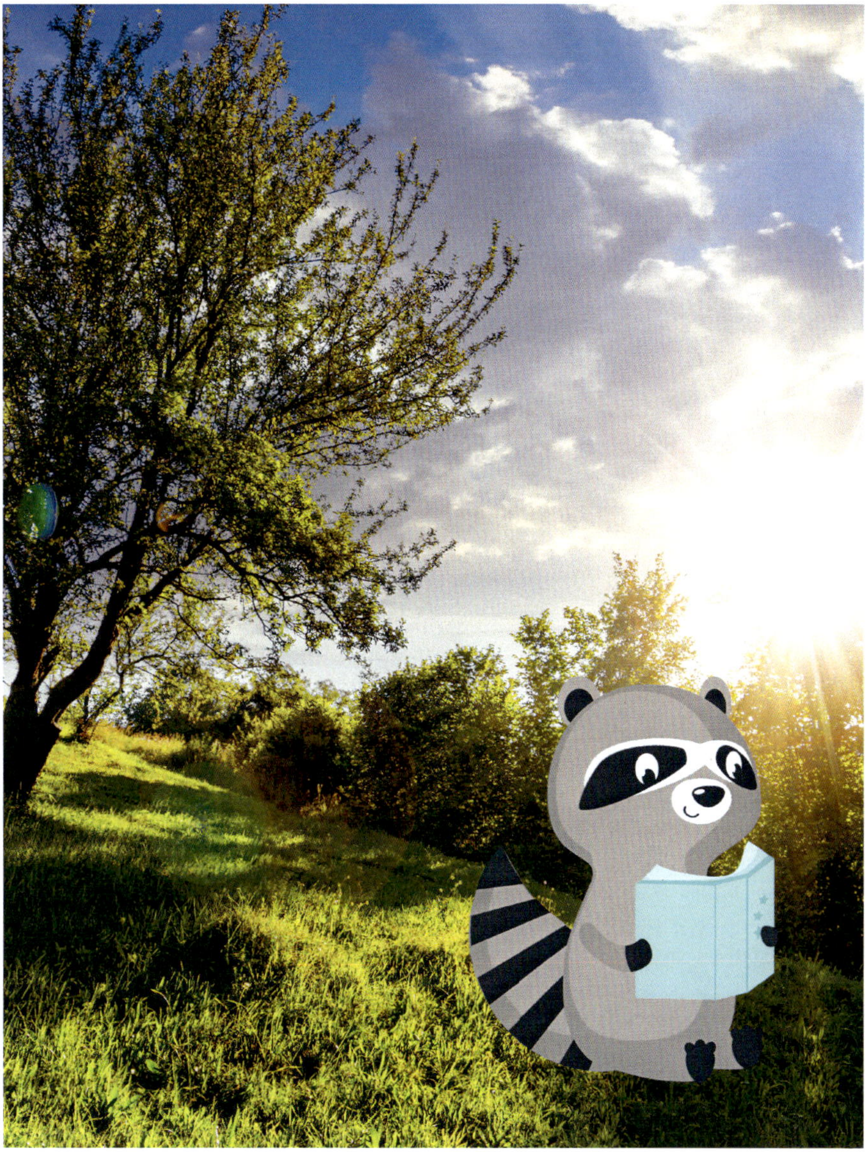

35

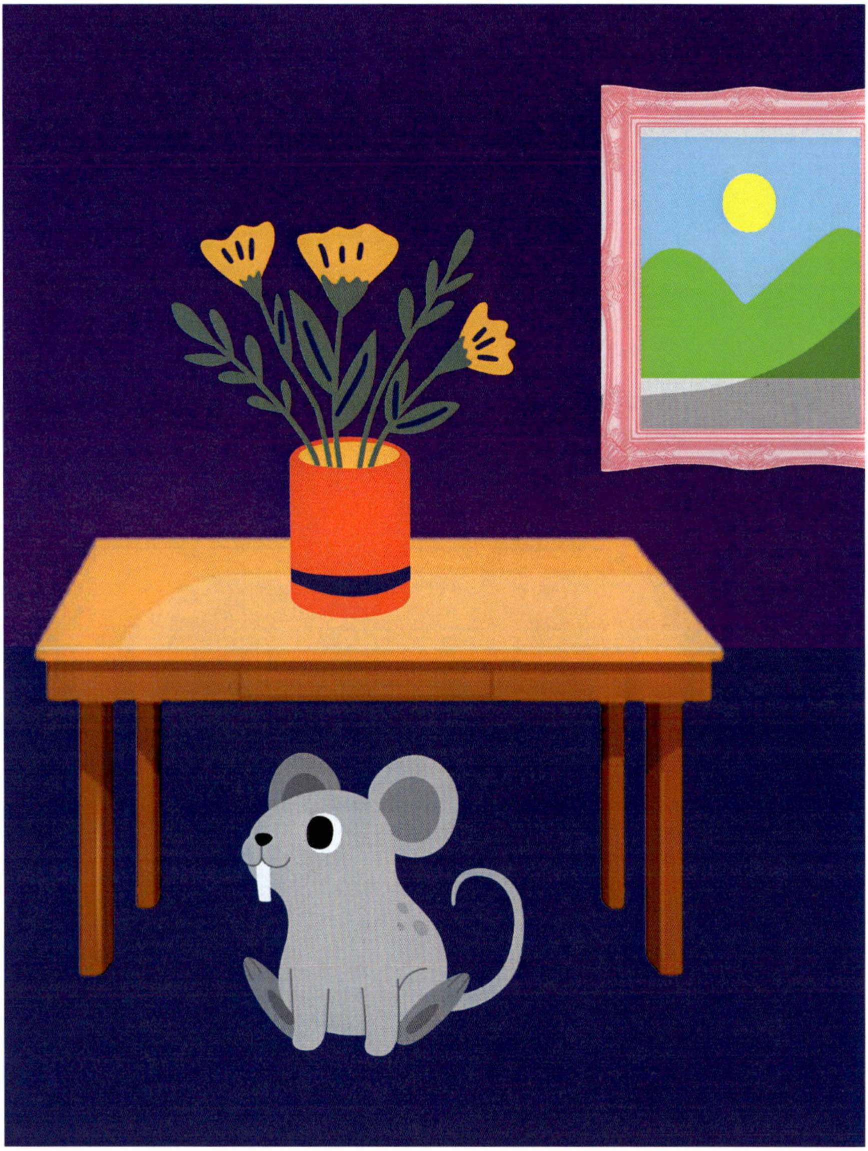

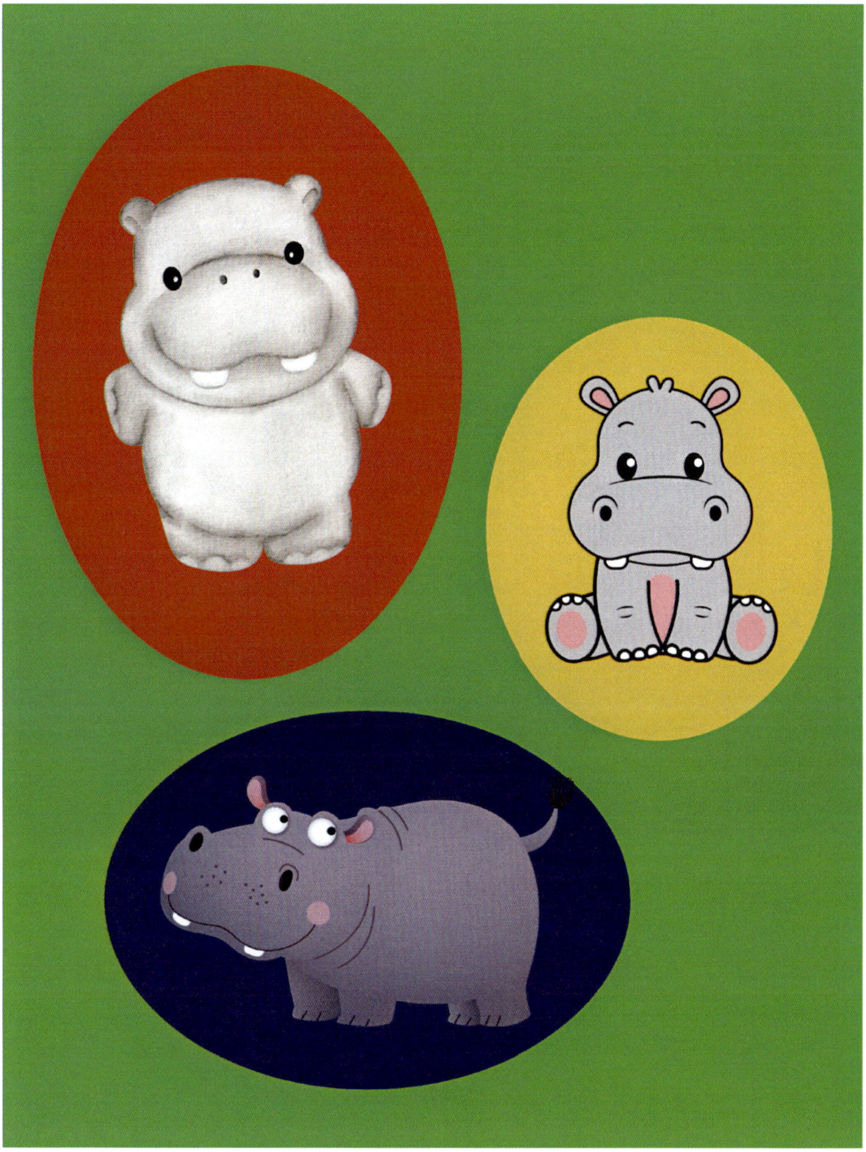

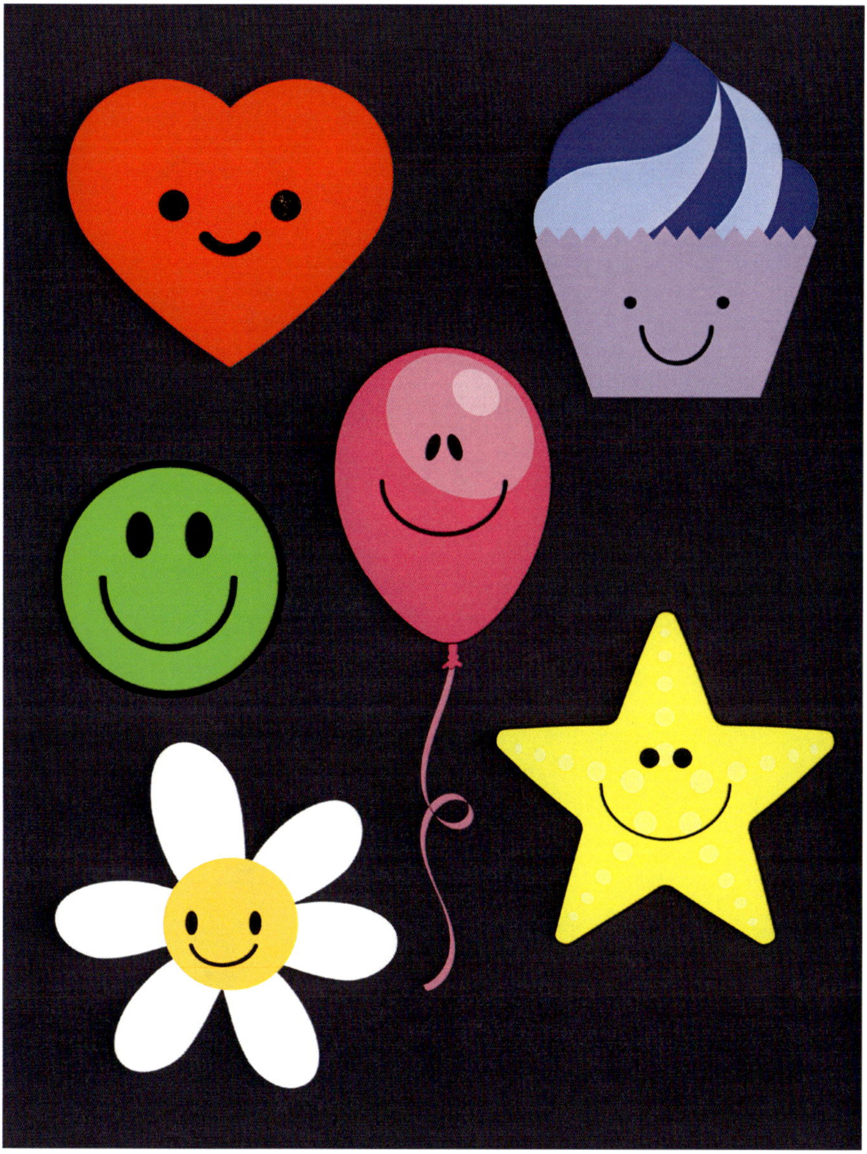

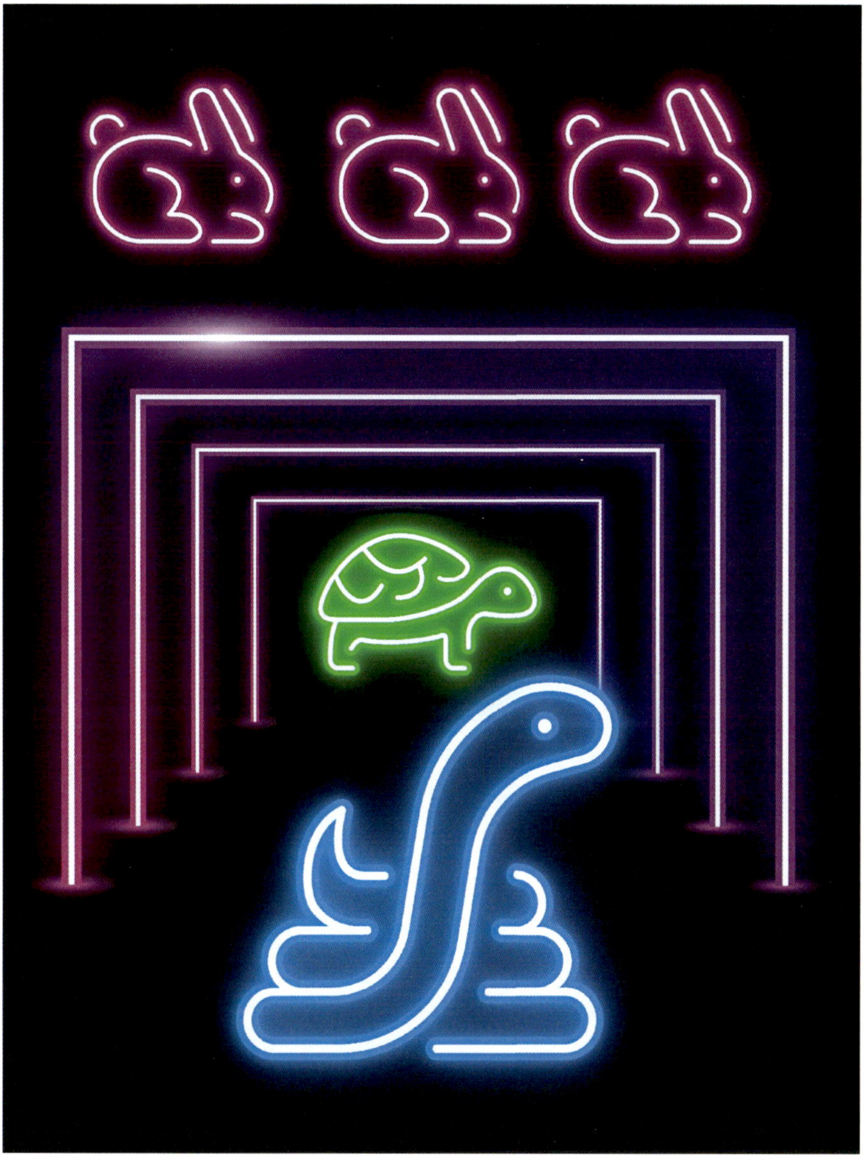

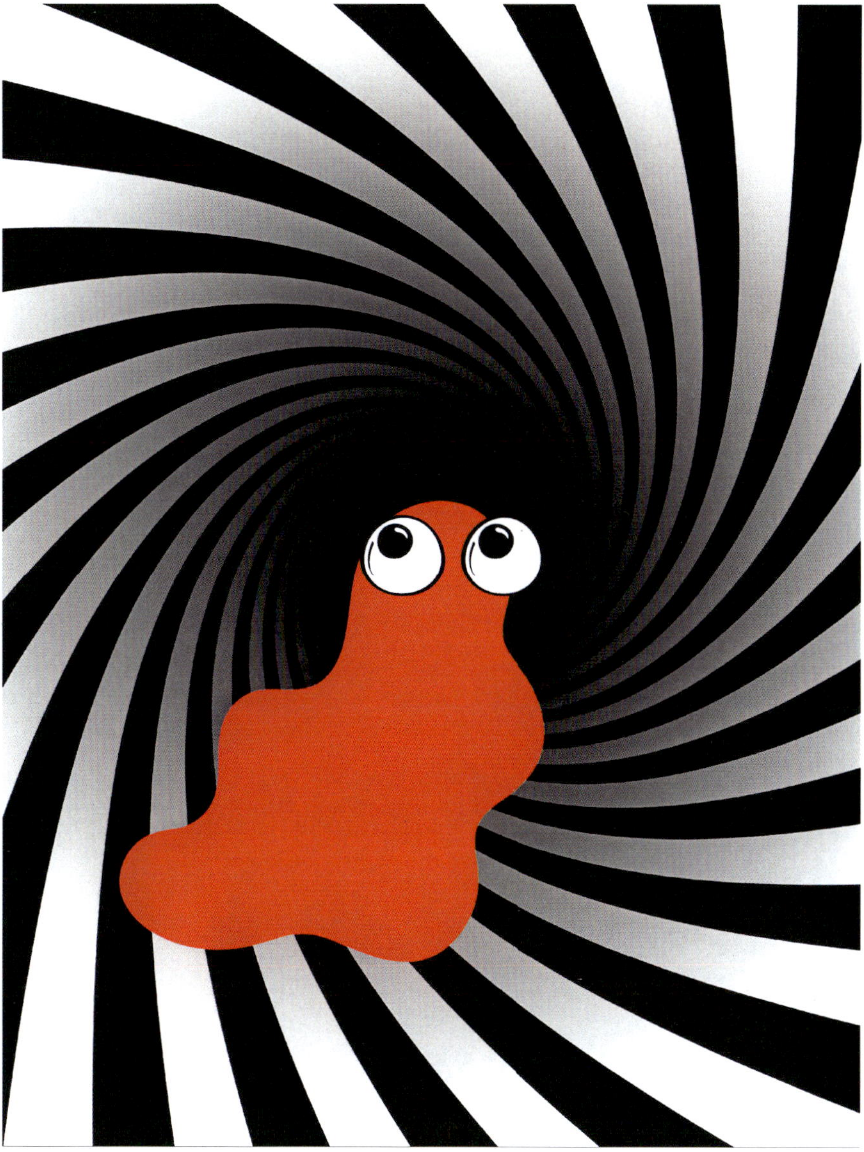

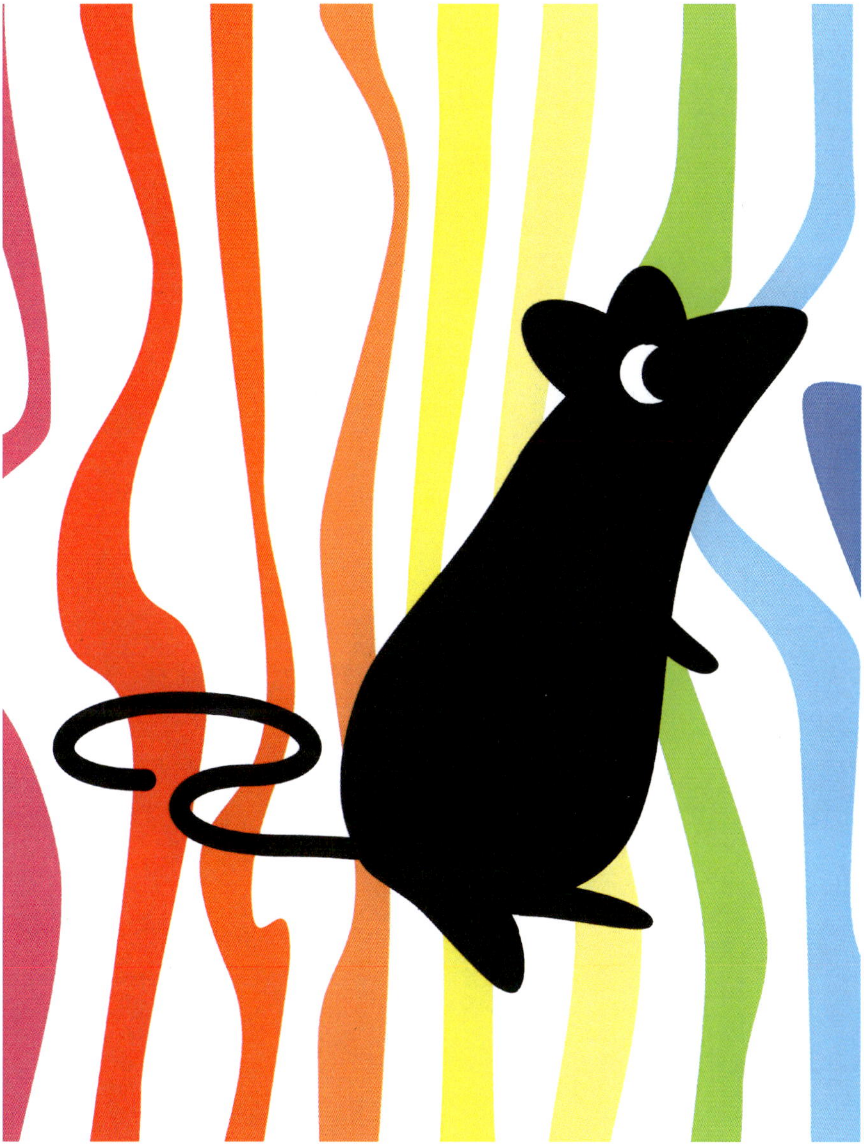

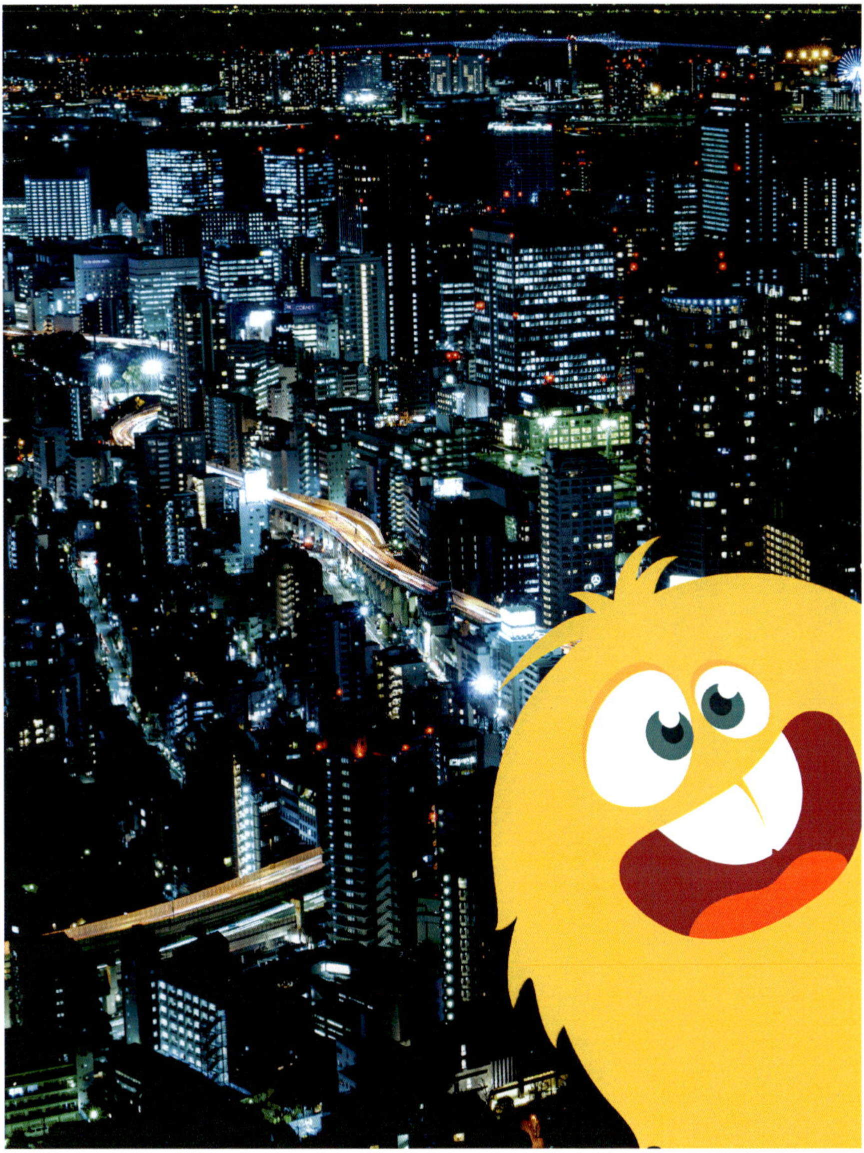

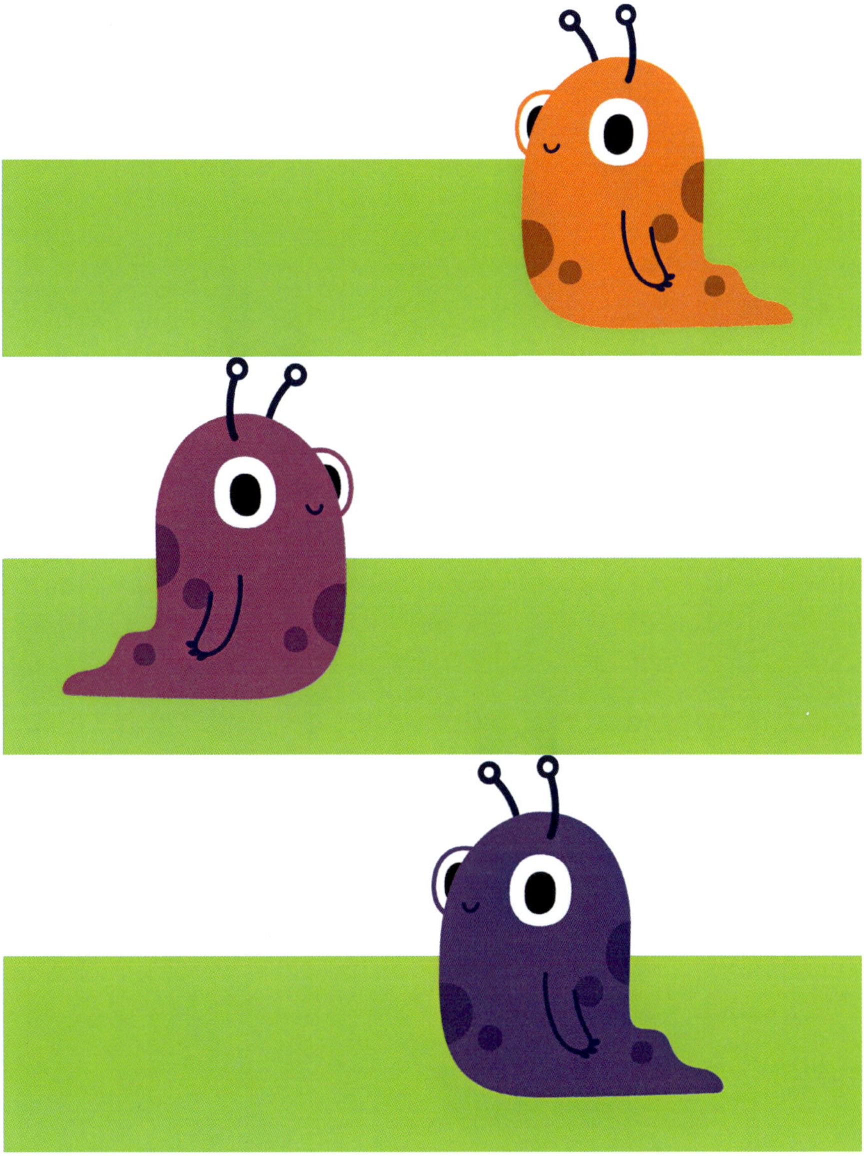

Stories for Youngsters

Pet Shop

In a cage at a pet shop, there were a whole bunch of soft bunnies. People came in all the time and bought bunnies. Everyone loved to pick up the rabbits and pet their soft fur. Next to the rabbits was a cage with a prickly hedgehog in it. He longed to be petted but no one ever picked him up to cuddle with him because of his rough spines. He watched sadly as people kept petting the bunnies and kept buying them to take home and pet them some more. Then, one day, a dirty family came in the store. It was a mom, a dad, and a boy. The boy was scratching all over because fleas made him itch. He went straight to the hedgehog and picked him up. He rubbed the hedgehog all over his arms and used it to scratch his stomach. "Ahh, that feels much better," said the boy. "Ahh," said the hedgehog. It felt good to him, too. The boy told his mom and dad that he had found the pet he wanted. He took the hedgehog home and everyone was happy.

The Rooms

A nanny was watching two children, Ralph and Alfred, whose father was at work. Each child had a room of his own. The nanny told them to spend the afternoon cleaning their rooms. Ralph quickly threw all of his clothes into the hamper, all of his toys into the toybox, his papers and drawings into his desk, and anything else lying around under the bed. The room didn't look perfect, but it looked pretty clean pretty fast. He was happy that he was able to clean up so fast, and he spent his remaining time laying on his bed reading. Alfred already had a bunch of stuff under his bed, so he pulled it all out to go through it. His toy box was full, and everything in it was a mess, so he took everything out and tried to sort through it. His papers and drawings were already in his desk, but he got them out so he could put them in categories and make sure his desk was neat inside. Toward the end of the day, before the boys' father got home, the nanny came in to inspect the rooms. She came to the room that was clean, and said, "Good job, Ralph. Your father will be proud. Why don't you go to the kitchen and have some pudding." But when she came to the Alfred's room, it was a disaster. There were stacks of paper all over the floor, piles of clothes everywhere, and toys all around the toybox. "This is a mess! You did not do what I asked you to do. No pudding for you. You should be ashamed." The child looked around at his mess and felt despair. How could he ever clean it before his father got home?
Later, his father got home. The nanny told him she asked the boys to clean their rooms. The father saw the clean room, and then he saw the messy room. He said "fellas, you both have a lot more work to do. Alfred, I am glad your mess is out in the open. I may need for you to help your brother since you are so far ahead."

The Scared Little Tea Cup

Once, there was a little tea cup that hid in the back of the cupboard because he was scared that if someone used him, he might get dropped or broken. He was bright blue and didn't want to get even a crack in him. Each time the cabinet would open, he scooted to the back.

The other tea cups encouraged him to not be afraid. "You won't get broken," they said. One of the other tea cups corrected them. "Actually, you might get broken," he said. "You really might. But is that worse than never being used?"

The tea cup thought about it and, shaking, moved to the front. The next time the cabinet door opened, the lady picked him and filled him with hot cinnamon tea. It felt good. All of a sudden, the tea cup felt himself falling. His worst fears were coming true. He smashed into the ground and broke into bits.

"Oh, no," he heard the lady say. The tea cup realized that he had fallen, but he felt okay. He felt the lady pick up all the little bits. But instead of being thrown in the trashcan, he was washed off and taken to another room and put in a bowl. The next day, the lady took all of his pieces, mixed him with other pieces of broken pottery, and made a mosaic flower pot out of them. She set the flower pot on her porch, and every time guests came over, they complimented the lady on her flower pot. People raved and raved about the beautiful pattern made by the pottery pieces. The tea cup felt so happy to be with other broken tea cup friends together in a piece of art.

The Magic Pillow

　　Ralph Ralpherson had an okay life. He had a job and some friends. Sometimes he took walks. One day, he was taking a walk down the street, and he came upon a store called "The Mysterious Store." "Hmmm," he thought. "Now that's kind of mysterious." He went in, and it was a brightly lit shop that looked kind of like a thrift store, except much more mysterious. There were all kinds of trinkets, accessories, appliances, games, and hats and things on shelves. The shopkeeper greeted him. "Hello, welcome to the mysterious store," he said to Ralph.
　　"Hi," said Ralph. "I'm just looking."
　　Ralph noticed a blue and white striped pillow that said "Magic Dream Pillow, 5 dollars."
　　"What does this pillow do?" asked Ralph.
　　"It gives you good dreams," said the man. He seemed friendly.
　　"I'll try it out," said Ralph, handing the man five dollars.
　　Ralph bought the pillow and went home. That night, he dreamt the best dream he had ever had. He dreamt he was on a hill flying a kite with loved ones, and afterward they went out to get ice cream, and he bought ice cream for everyone in sight.
　　When he woke up the next day, he wanted to go back to sleep to have another dream. Somehow, he managed to go to work, but all day, he thought about getting back home to the pillow.
　　The pillow always gave him good dreams, and he began using all his free time sleeping. He didn't have time for friends anymore, and he even started showing up to work late. Eventually, he didn't show up to work at all, and he got fired. All he wanted to do was dream. As he spent his life dreaming, his real life became a nightmare. He had unpaid bills, angry neighbors, no job, and no companionship. One day, he forced himself to go back to the store. He didn't bring the pillow with him, because he didn't want the man to take it.

"Hi," he said to the man. "I am having problems. I can't stop sleeping on this pillow." What should I do?"

The man looked at him compassionately. "Take a walk once a day," he said. "I will help you with the rest."

Ralph did as he was told. Each day, during the walk, the man would come replace the dream pillow with a pillow that gave dreams that weren't as good. The dreams gradually got worse and worse. The shopkeeper kept switching out pillows until he had finally replaced the pillow with a nightmare pillow. Ralph started dreaming of fanged creatures and situations where he felt ashamed. He could barely endure sleeping on the pillow anymore, and he spent as little time at home as possible.

He called his old friends and asked them to spend time with him. They did. He also found a new job and worked hard to take his mind off the nightmares. There, he met some new friends, and a girl named Ralphette, who he liked. He told her about the nightmares.

"Why don't you take the pillow back?" she said. Ralph did, and the shopkeeper even gave him his five dollars back because of his bad experience. From then on, Ralph slept on a regular pillow. He married Ralphette, they had kids, and they spent their Saturdays flying kites and eating ice cream, which Ralph shared with everyone in sight as an expression of gratitude for his best dreams coming true.

Color Scheme

One day, there was a king who decided to play a practical joke on the child that he and his wife were expecting. He wanted his child to grow up without knowing about the color yellow. He decided that when she turned ten, he would show her yellow things and it would be a surprise. Until then, he issued a decree banning the color yellow from their land and telling all the people to get rid of anything they had that was yellow. People had to destroy flower beds, break vases, throw away art, repaint their houses, burn clothes, and dye hair. The king even assigned a group of woodsmen to make sure nothing yellow grew in the forest or in the meadows. No one was allowed to mention the color, either. There was also a curfew so no one would be outside during sunsets and sunrises. That way, if there were yellow streaks, no one would see them and find out. Within a few years, many people had forgotten about it. The other children born the same year as the king's child didn't know about the color, either. A few weeks before the child's tenth birthday, the king ordered thousands of gallons of yellow paint and had the townspeople paint everything in the kingdom yellow. The king thought it was hilarious. When he woke up the next day, though, he found that everything had been painted yellow with purple polka dots. Even the animals were painted. His child was amazed, and the joke worked, but the king was also amazed. You see, his own father had played a similar practical joke on him and had kept purple a secret from him for his whole life. The king was kind of amused and kind of mad.

The Photographer Who Got Followed Around By A Green And Yellow Bird

Once, there was a photographer named Ralph Ralpherson. He loved to take pictures of mountains, flowers, buildings, and anything outside, whether it was man-made or natural. He spent hours trying to get the right angle and set up his shots.

To Ralph's dismay, there happened to be a green and yellow bird that followed him around and snuck into every photo that Ralph took. Whenever Ralph had photo exhibits or showed people albums of his photos, people would say, "Oh, wow, I like your bird pictures." This frustrated Ralph.

Finally, at one exhibit, a lady came up to him and said, "These are the most beautiful pictures of buildings and mountains and flowers that I have ever seen. And putting the bird in the background is a cool way to sign them." Ralph cried, and they got married.

The Woodcarver

There was once a kingdom with a great wooden wall around it. Everyone in the kingdom had his own special job to perform. One man, Ralph Ralpherson, was a wood carver. He loved to carve beautiful designs into wooden plates, bowls, boxes, and furniture. He carved wooden animals for all of the children, too. He worked for years to improve his skill and loved to bless others with his talent. Unfortunately, some people did not appreciate his efforts. Some of the parents didn't want their kids playing with the wooden lions and tigers Ralph gave them, because they thought their kids might end up playing with real lions and tigers and get eaten. People also got annoyed when little bits of food got caught in the grooves of the plates and bowls that Ralph had carved. The king finally summoned Ralph into his throne room and told Ralph that he was banished from the kingdom forever. Ralph cried, but left willingly. Outside the kingdom, he looked at the wooden walls. He still loved the kingdom, and he decided to show his devotion by carving designs into the walls. He spent days and days carving intricate designs into the wood. He carved entire scenes from the kingdom's favorite literature. He carved gardens and zoos into some panels. He carved pictures of the mountains and rivers that surrounded the kingdom. It was a work of art. Unfortunately, as he was putting his finishing touches on one of the wall corners, a guard discovered him and turned him in. He was driven further away. In the woods surrounding the kingdom, he began carving into the trees. He wanted anyone from the kingdom who took a walk or rode a horse in the forest to get to enjoy his carving. He carved places for people to hide food and treasures. He carved ladders into trees so people could climb up and look at the kingdom. He made treehouses and carved ornate designs on their walls and stairways. Unfortunately, a hunter from the kingdom discovered his work and drove him further away into a desert. Ralph managed to survive, and used rocks to carve designs into the bark of what shrubs and trees he could find. He cried every day, remembering his love for his kingdom, and he carved pictures of the people he had known. One day, as he sat in the shade of one of the few trees, he saw a man coming toward him. When the man got closer, Ralph noticed that he was wearing colorful overalls unlike any Ralph had ever seen, and he was carrying something in his hand. The man finally arrived at the tree and held out what he was carrying. It was a wooden lizard that Ralph had carved out of a cactus trunk.

"Did you carve this?" the man said.

"Yes," said Ralph. "You can keep it. I would love it if you kept it."

"Come with me," said the man in the colorful overalls.

Ralph did not know who the man was, but he had already carved all the wood he could find, so he had nothing better to do, and he decided to follow the man.

The man in the colorful overalls led him through the desert to a canyon. On the other side of the canyon, there was an opening to a cave, and Ralph followed the man inside. The cave was lined with torches, and there was a river that ran through it. Ralph and the man got in a wooden boat and began rowing through the cave.

"I would love to carve this boat." said Ralph.

"You will," said the man.

Ralph's heart smiled. He knew that something good was happening.

Soon, Ralph could see a beam of light ahead of him. They got to the end of the cave and Ralph's eyes adjusted to the radiant light. All around them was a beautiful kingdom of houses made of every kind of wood in the world. There were windmills and lighthouses and waterwheels, too. There were people in overalls walking around everywhere. A few smiled and waved. The man in the overalls turned to Ralph.

"We would like for you to be in our kingdom and carve wood for us," he said.

Ralph started crying and looked around to figure out where to start.

A Story About A Bunch of Guys Who Argued A Lot

A whole bunch of guys decided to argue in a room. They were arguing loudly about what was true in the world. They argued for days, taking as few breaks as possible so they wouldn't accidentally let someone else convince the others of something they didn't believe. They shouted and shouted, sometimes changing their minds, but were never able to fully agree about anything. Finally, one guy left and came back. He painted all of the walls blue and said to the others, "Let us agree that these walls are blue."

"They are blue, indeed," said one of the men.

"I agree," said another.

"Well said," shouted another.

All of the men started nodding in agreement and marveling at how blue the walls were.

"We must share our discovery with others," said a man whose voice was very hoarse from arguing.

The men left the room to tell everyone they could find about how blue the walls were.

Orange Soda

There aren't very many places more beautiful than the inside of a grocery store. Where else can you be surrounded by shelves and shelves of candy, cookies, chips, ice cream, and best of all, soda? Can you blame seven-year-old Ralph Ralpherson for wanting his mom to buy everything in sight?

"Sorry, Ralph," his mom said. "I'm only buying stuff that's good for you."

"Marshmallow double fudge fruit-tastic berrylicious cake bites are good for me," said Ralph.

His mom ignored him.

Aisle after aisle, Ralph presented groceries to his mom, hoping that at least one delicious treat would make it into the basket.

When Ralph picked up a bottle of orange soda, his mom snapped.

"No, Ralph. How many times do I have to say it? We're sticking to the list. Put it back."

"Fine," said Ralph, pouting.

But he didn't put the soda back. Instead, when his mom was deciding what brand of apple juice to buy, Ralph snuck the soda into the shopping cart. He put the bottle under a big bag of spinach so his mom wouldn't notice.

Mrs. Ralpherson didn't notice. In fact, she didn't even notice when the cashier rang up the soda and put it in the bag! And she still didn't notice when they got home and Ralph took the soda out of the grocery bag and snuck it to his room. Ralph couldn't believe that he had gotten away with it!!

That night, after dinner, Ralph pulled out the soda and took it to his bathroom to pour himself a cup. Unfortunately, the heavy bottle slipped as he was pouring it, and a lot of the soda went down the drain. Ralph cleaned up the mess, drank a little, and hid the almost empty bottle.

He didn't think about the soda again until later when he was getting ready for bed. He turned on the faucet to rinse his toothbrush, and something amazing happened.

The "water" was orange and fizzy! Ralph turned off the faucet in disbelief. He turned it back on and sure enough, orange soda came gushing out.

He went and checked the bathtub's faucet. Once again, orange soda poured out. Ralph tasted it. Yep. It was the same soda he had tasted earlier.

He went to bed feeling a little uneasy that night.

"Wake up, Ralph!"

Was it morning already?

"You won't believe what has happened!" Mrs. Ralpherson said. "Your father got in the shower this morning, and the water was orange! It tastes like soda. He went to work a little sticky!"

Ralph couldn't believe this was happening.

"I called the neighbors and their water is like that too!" his mom said.

On the school bus, everyone was talking about the soda. It seemed that everyone's water had turned into orange soda. Ralph looked out the window and watched the sprinklers spraying orange soda all over the lawns. He wished he could be excited about it like everyone else, but he was worried. He knew that this must have something to do with the soda he spilled.

At school, all of the kids were lined up at the water fountain (now an orange soda fountain), a little thirstier than usual. Ralph frowned. What if all of the water in the world had turned to orange soda? People in Venice, Italy would be boating on orange soda. Big Ben in London would be overlooking a river of soda. China's rivers would flood with the orange soda. Even Niagra Falls would turn into orange soda!

When Ralph got home from school that day, his mom was watching the news. The mayor was addressing the city.

"We still don't know what happened," said the mayor. "It seems that all of the city's water turned to orange soda overnight."

"Can you believe this?" Ralph's mom asked him. "I've never seen anything like it. But I must say, it is very good soda."

The mayor continued. "The orange soda is safe to drink, but we do have scientists at the water treatment plant working to change it back to water. The TV showed the orange soda all over town. Even the river in the city had changed colors. Luckily, there was a dam to keep the soda from spreading to other cities, and the ducks didn't seem to mind too much.

The mayor came back on the screen. "We need to know where the soda came from," he said. "If we know the ingredients and where this soda came from, we can figure out what happened."

"Mom," said Ralph. Tears formed in his eyes. "I need to show you something." He went to his room to get the half-empty soda bottle. He sobbed as he told his mom the whole story.

"I'm glad you told me," his mom said. "Let's take this bottle downtown."

The mayor was grateful when Ralph and his mom brought the bottle to his office. Within a few days, the people in charge of the water system had figured out how to pump clean water back into the system. The mayor also took the bottle to the grocery store to make sure they didn't order any more like that.

The grocery store manager was dumbfounded.

"Sir," he said. " This is not a brand that we normally carry. I don't know where it came from."

No one ever really figured out where that bottle had come from or what had made it change everything to orange soda, but one thing was for sure: Ralph had certainly learned his lesson. Next time, he would get a bottle of grape soda.

The Magic Pen

One day, this guy named Ralph Ralpherson was at a rummage sale and found a pen that said "Magic Pen" on it. He was excited, and took it home to start writing. He wrote some poems and essays and showed them to people he knew. They were utterly amazed at how inspirational and beautiful the poems and essays were. He kept writing, and all of his essays and poems were published and widely read. People couldn't believe what heartfelt love and kindness was expressed in Ralph's writing. The critics wrote that Ralph's essays and poetry contained "healing words of love and light that warm the soul." Everyone marveled at how pure and gentle Ralph's tone was, and how generous and forgiving his attitude toward humanity seemed. Ralph kind of enjoyed the praise, but he felt a little uneasy, because the package that the pen had come in said that it was magic because as you write with it, it writes the opposite of what you really think.

The Carpet Pattern

Once, a guy named Ralph was staring at the oriental carpet in his living room and realized its pattern was very interesting. He decided to start telling guests that it was a treasure map, and no one had found the treasure yet because they hadn't been able to interpret the pattern. He told them the treasure was very valuable with lot of gold coins involved. Most of his guests believed him, and they kept coming up with excuses to visit Ralph and study the pattern. People started bringing over snacks to share with everyone. Ralph's living room became the neighborhood hangout. Everyone tried to be nice to each other instead of fiercely competitive because they wanted to be invited back. They would draw sketches of the carpet and go off to distant lands to try finding the treasure. Ralph's guests, many of them neighbors, and many from far away as well, got to know each other very well. They traded stories and secrets while drawing copies of the rug and comparing the pattern to other maps from books they had found.

One day, a man stopped sketching and said, "Hey, Ralph, you know what? You know what I think the treasure is? I think the treasure is our friendship. I think the treasure is the fun that we all have being here."

Ralph smiled, and was about to tell everyone that the carpet pattern thing was really a joke, but right then, one of the treasure hunters burst through the door and poured a bag of gold coins out over the carpet. "I found it!" he said. "I found the treasure. The map worked! Help yourself, everyone! The treasure was in the woods next to the neighborhood and there are hundreds more bags of gold just like this!"

Everyone was amazed, but Ralph even more than the rest of them.

FloopyDoo Story

Once upon a time, in a land far away, there was a kingdom where everyone loved food. They loved food so much that they had fancy huge food parties with hundreds of different choices. Breakfast, lunch, and dinner would all take two hours each, and they added two more meals a day so they could eat leftovers. Unfortunately, this took a lot of work to prepare, and it took even more work to clean up. But one day, literally out of the clear blue sky, all of these beautiful balloons fell slowly upon the village and castle. There were hundreds and hundreds of them. Inside the balloons were red, yellow, and blue furry creatures with googly eyes and long arms. They didn't have legs, but instead just bounced and floated wherever they went. The people decided to call the creatures "floopydoos." The people soon figured out that the little creatures were very helpful. The red ones liked to cook, the yellow ones liked to clean, and the blue ones went around giving people compliments. Perfect! But who would get to keep them? The king decided that each person could have one floopydoo per mistake that they had made in their lives.

This was great news to some people, because they had made a lot of mistakes. There was one guy who had failed every class at school and had accidentally burned down three of his own houses. He told the king all about his mistakes, and he wound up with eight hundred floopydoos. His banquets became the most popular in the kingdom. At each banquet, the people got to taste food that they had never tried before. But this did not happen for everyone. Some people didn't want anyone to know that they had made mistakes, so they did not admit that they had. They only got one or two floopydoos, and some people, who wanted others to think that they were perfect, got none at all.

Eventually all the people who had pretended to be perfect figured out that they had made a mistake by doing that. And when they admitted it, the king gave them some of the green floopydoos that told jokes. They had been kept a secret. The king saved them for the people with the biggest mistakes.

It's a Small Universe After All

Once, there was a kid named Ralph, and his parents bought a transporter portal generator one year. If they clicked a button on the remote control, it projected a round glowing portal that they could step through to be anywhere in the universe. They just had to set the dial on the remote control first. Ralph was not allowed to use it unless he was with his parents, and he was frustrated because his parents only used it to go to the grocery store and back. They never used it for anything else, and even on vacation, they just took the car to the beach instead of going through the portal to visit other cool planets and worlds. Ralph asked them why, and they said that it was so valuable to be able to go to the grocery store so easily that they didn't want to risk using it to go anywhere else, because what if it broke?

One day, Ralph decided to take the portal and go to a far-off place without permission. He set the dial to a high-up number and walked through the glowing hole. He found himself in the grocery store of another planet. There were smooth, blue, googly-eyed aliens all around him with shopping carts, and they were filling them up with different kinds of foods that Ralph had never seen before. Most of the foods either made noise or glowed. The creatures were surprised to see him. One blue mom with two little blue kids came up to him and welcomed him to the grocery store. The portal generator translated her language for him.

"Welcome," she said. "I am so happy that my children get to see an alien. It is a treat for all of us."

"Thanks," said Ralph.

The alien kept talking to him. "I must tell you that I am surprised, though, to see that you have used your portal to come to our planet. Here, we only use our portals to go to the grocery store, because we believe that it is unwise to risk breaking it by going anywhere else. I advise you to do the same, young alien."

"Yes, ma'am," said Ralph. He set the dial to go home, walked through the portal back into his home, and never broke the rules again.

The Lost Stones of Greydorn

When Ralph Ralpherson was in fifth grade, his class was doing some science experiments with volcanoes, and they made volcanoes that shot out a whole bunch of red paint. Ralph went to go wash off the paint in the bathroom, but when he opened the little door to the restroom, it wasn't the restroom that had always been there. Instead, there was a staircase of stone steps that went far down and turned the corner, and there was light coming from beyond where they turned. Ralph decided to see where they led. He was just going to see where the light was coming from and then turn around and go back to class, but when he did turn around, the bathroom was gone. Ralph realized he was standing on the stone staircase with no railing, and it was really high up in the air, and below him was some land and water. Ralph was very scared, but he also thought it was cool, so he kept going, even as he realized that the stairs were disappearing behind him. The air was filled with some googly-eyed birds that were really cute and helped him feel less frightened.

Ralph finally got to the bottom and found himself in a meadow full of flowers. There was a trail cutting through the flowers so he followed it to the edge of some woods. Just then, an old wizard wearing a red cloak and holding a puppy walked up to Ralph. He handed Ralph the puppy and said, "Here, child. Hold this puppy and you will be able to calm down." Ralph held the puppy and felt much better.

"Where am I?" Ralph asked.

"I cannot tell you that," the wizard said. "I cannot tell you the name of this land. All I can tell you is that you have an important mission, and all of the people in this land, and all of the creatures everywhere are counting on you to do it."

"A mission?"

"Yes," said the wizard. "A quest. Follow me."

Ralph followed him, holding the puppy. It was brown and white and very cute.

The wizard finally stopped in front of a huge tree, and behind the tree, Ralph could see another staircase. The very sight of it made him scared because of what had just happened with the other staircase.

"Is this one going to take us to another land?" Ralph asked.

"No," he said. "It will take us into the Cave of Greydorn. You are safe. I promise."

Inside the cave, there were some round lights just floating through the air, slowly moving and lighting up the whole place. There were bookshelves everywhere, filled with books, and some other tables and shelves with mysterious looking bottles, artwork, and wooden boxes. In the middle of the room stood a small well. It looked just like those wishing wells you always find in stories.

There were ratty, poofy chairs scattered around the room, and the wizard told Ralph to have a seat.

"Everyone has been expecting you," he said. "We are counting on you. If you are not willing to help us, I will understand, and I will help you get home. But if you are willing, you would help our whole kingdom."

Ralph really wanted to go home, but he asked the wizard what he needed anyway.

"It may be a dangerous mission, and it may take many days. There are five magic stones that must be collected from this land. They have been hidden, and we need someone to find them and bring them back to me so I can put them in this well. When I throw them in this well, everyone in the kingdom will be set free from the curse of Greydorn. There may be one past the mountain range in the distance, but that area is very dangerous. There are many wild animals and enemies."

The wizard got out a map of the land and started showing Ralph possible locations of the stones.

"No one knows where they are," he said. "We need someone to find them. According to legend, one is blue, one is red, one is yellow, one is green, and one is purple. They are small and smooth, and warm to the touch."

"Do they look like those stones?" Ralph asked, shifting the puppy to one arm and pointing to a pile of colorful stones next to a pottery bowl.

The wizard looked over at the shelf and gasped. "The lost stones of Greydorn! That's right. I forgot that I already had them! That other kid found them for me a couple of years ago. I just forgot to put them in the well!"

The wizard picked them up with both of his hands, went over to the well, and dropped them all in. There was a low rumble that sounded like it came from far away, and the room shook a little bit. Then it was quiet again.

"I'm so sorry to trouble you," the big wizard said. "I forgot that I had already collected the stones. Our kingdom will be fine. I hope that this has not been an inconvenience."

"No, it's okay," Ralph said. I don't mind." Ralph started to give the puppy back to the wizard.

"Keep the puppy," he said. "You can have it. Here, let me show you how to get back home." He led Ralph to a door and opened it. Outside the door, Ralph could see his school hallway. He wanted to go through, but he didn't really know how he would explain the puppy thing to his teacher. He decided to keep the puppy and just tell her the truth.

"Thanks for the puppy," Ralph said to the wizard.

"You're welcome," he said. "Sorry to bother you."

"It's okay. Bye."

Ralph took the puppy back to class, and though his teacher didn't believe him and called his parents, he did end up getting to keep the dog, who turned out to be the best pet ever.

The Magic Pants

Ralph Ralpherson was just living his regular life when a traveling salesman came to his town and put up a sign saying "Magic Pants For Sale." All of the pants he was selling were plaid. He set up a stage near his booth and had his five children dancing together to music from all different cultures. Four of them were wearing plaid pants, and one of them was wearing just regular jeans. The four who were wearing the plaid pants danced better than anyone had ever seen. They all danced in rhythm and did flips and dips that seemed physically impossible to the people who watched and marveled. The fifth child who was wearing regular jeans struggled to keep up. He didn't seem to have as much rhythm as the others, and he often stumbled, sometimes falling all the way down.

"Wow, those pants really work!" exclaimed the onlookers. "I want to be able to dance like that!!"

In just a few days, the salesman sold out of magic pants. Ralph couldn't believe how many people had fallen for that guy's scheme. He was glad that he was smart enough not to waste money on ordinary pants. Ralph still thought that he was a clever businessman, though, and he went to tell him so as he packed up his booth.

"Well, I must admit that you are a clever guy," Ralph said. "That is a pretty clever way to sell a lot of pants."

"Oh, I'm not that clever," he said. "I am this successful because I have a magic hat that I bought from a traveling salesman a long time ago." The man tipped his plaid hat to Ralph and shuffled off.

Good Weather

Ralphette Ralpherson had always wished that it would rain candy. She wished that there would be candy storms where lollipops and peppermints and chocolates and all kinds of other candy would just fall from the sky, and people could take barrels and buckets and take them outside to collect the falling candy. As Ralphette grew older, she started to realize that it was very unlikely that it would ever rain candy, and she decided that she would have to make candy fall from the sky herself. She went into business and saved lots and lots of money. She bought thousands of boxes of candy and got helicopter pilots to fly high over the sky of her city. Then, she had them drop candy for almost thirty minutes. Tons of candy fell all over the city. Some people got hurt, but most people were happy.

"It's raining candy!" they shouted. Most of them had also wished all their lives that it would rain candy, and they were so happy and amazed that their wish was coming true. The people who got hurt complained, though, and Ralphette was told not to drop candy from the sky ever again. She agreed not to.

But a few months later, candy started falling from the sky again, and the police immediately arrested Ralphette.
"But I didn't arrange this!" said Ralphette. Turns out it was really raining candy. It was a candy front that had been caused by warm air in the gulf moving over cooler ocean currents. When everyone realized that it really was raining candy, Ralphette didn't have to go to jail after all. Instead, everyone collected the candy in barrels and saved it for a sunny day.

Light Story

    The sun was tired of shining. He said so.
    "Quit whining," said the moon. But really, the moon felt sorry for the sun. The sun had been shining for a long time.
    "Why don't you take a day off?" the moon asked the sun.
    "Who will light the sky?" asked the sun.
    "Trust me," said the moon, and he went to make a phone call.
    The next day, the sun got up to light the sky and saw that it was already lit. He looked closer to see where the light was coming from. All of the fireflies in the world had lit up and were holding it for a day.
    "Thank you," the sun said. He spent his day off laying out at the beach.

Refried Bean
is from Greenville, SC
and writes stories and jokes,
poems, and art books for
people of all ages, especially
the young at heart or sad.